IT TAKES AN EGG TIMER

IT TAKES AN EGG TIMER

A GUIDE TO CREATING THE
TIME FOR YOUR LIFE

Joanne Tombrakos

It Takes an Egg Timer
Joanne Tombrakos

Cover design: Wendy Bass
Interior design: Jamie Kerry for Belle Étoile Studios

Print edition ISBN 978-0-9840076-3-9
Kindle edition ISBN 978-0-9840076-4-6

Printed and bound in the United States of America

To my mother
and her ever-faithful egg timer

"Your time is limited, so don't waste it living someone else's life. Don't be trapped by dogma—which is living with the results of other people's thinking. Don't let the noise of other's opinions drown out your own inner voice. And most important, have the courage to follow your heart and intuition. They somehow already know what you truly want to become. Everything else is secondary."

—Steve Jobs

Introduction

One of the biggest excuses for not creating the change we want is that we are convinced we just don't have the time. We're already on overload. How can we possibly fit one more thing in? We're convinced we have not a moment to do those things we have to do, much less what we yearn most to do.

Time, we are certain, is an elusive entity; it moves too fast and slips through our fingers like grains of sand in an hourglass. We can't imagine that we can create any real change when we barely have enough hours in the day to do what is already filling our plate.

The irony is that when we do try to create something new, we start from this place of lack.

I wrote this to prove that excuse wrong. You do have enough time—for everything you have to and want to, and then some. It's just a question of what you are letting get in the way.

Be forewarned. This is not your typical book on time management. But you probably figured that out from the title. It's part guide and part manifesto. It will not be boring. It will not be filled with a thousand statistics and include a big appendix at the end.

It requires imagination and a willingness to experiment with my kitchen-tested ideas that may seem silly or irreverent at times, and at others, more spiritual than pragmatic.

Its genesis began when I left the corporate world almost four years ago. I've always had a reputation for having a good handle on my time, for being organized, driven, and for getting a lot more accomplished in any given day than the average person. But now, left without the aide of someone else's structure, I found myself newly challenged.

I had an advantage, a genetic predisposition to being a self-starter and twenty-five years of sales experience. No one can be successful in sales without the ability to manage oneself.

But I was still tested. This book is a result of that experience and is written for two groups.

It is for the self-employed and the entrepreneurs out there who struggle every day to keep themselves on task, productive, and happy.

It is also for those who simply dream about making a change in their life, big or small, but delude themselves that the reason they are not doing anything about it is that they just don't have the time.

So this is more than a guide. It's a manifesto that might just inspire you to see that the time does exist to create whatever is next for you—a new business, a book, a promotion, a new love, increased sales, or more lazy Saturday afternoons with your family. You get to choose. But first, you have to take a few moments out of that frenzied schedule to stop and read.

"Time is on my side—yes, it is."

—The Rolling Stones

My Endless Summers

The summers of my youth were a seemingly limitless series of days that stretched long after the sun went down. Our neighborhood on the fringe of the city in Queens was teeming with kids engaged in games of stoop ball or hopscotch on boards designed with colored chalk on the cement sidewalk. We collected fireflies in glass jars lined with pieces of grass while our parents kept watch, sitting on aluminum webbed beach chairs, smoking cigarettes, and drinking Rheingold beer, as they chose sides between the Mets and the Yankees. The night air was interrupted by the music of the occasional transistor radio or the jingles from Mr. Softee, Bungalow Bar, and the Good Humor ice cream trucks making their rounds. It was the sixties and though the outside world was full of social change and strife, those summers deluded us into believing time would always move this slowly and we would always have more of it than we could ever use.

Time as a commodity

Today that has all changed. Time has become precious and scarce. We live in fear of it slipping away too quickly for us to get anything done. Time is a commodity, one we try to harness. We equate time with productivity and money. We forget to set aside time for ourselves to just be and perhaps, even frivolously to have fun with.

The memories I shared of the lazy, hazy days of summer are a combination of those of a child and of a world that does not exist anymore. The average person's pace today is frenetic. Everyone is consumed with time, how to control it, how to have enough of it, and how to make the most of it.

We multi-task as though it were a badge of honor, barely taking the time to go for a walk in the park without our smartphones attached to our wrist, the way my mother used to attach my mittens to my winter coat. Even our youth is obsessed with it. Play does not occur organically with one child knocking on another's door to see if he or she wants to go ride bikes. It has morphed into scheduled play dates with a defined start and end. Wasting time is considered a puritanical sin that can send most of us to the confessional when we catch ourselves indulging.

"Lost time is never found again."

—Benjamin Franklin

Time as business

I used to sell time. Most people don't even know that you can do that, but there is an entire and very lucrative industry built around the buying and selling of this intangible. While you cannot wrap your hands around it, put it in a box, and tie it up with a ribbon, people like me have created careers selling this elusiveness we call time, that space of :30 or :60 in between the content on your favorite radio or television station that is filled with commercial copy.

My first advertising sales position was at WXTU, a then fledging country music radio station in Philadelphia. The urgency of what we did was impressed daily. We sold something that had a very short shelf life. If there were ten sixty-second allotments in the course of one hour of broadcast time and only five were sold, the leftovers did not accumulate in a warehouse to be sold later at markdown prices. Like the seats on an airplane, unsold inventory escapes into the ether, lost forever.

I learned a lot about the concept of time in those early experiences. For instance one hundred and fifty words is approximately how long it takes to fill :60 of radio copy. But more importantly, what became ingrained in me was the idea that time was money. In this case, literally. If I didn't make the most of it, I would lose the potential for cash in my pocket.

The urgency to not waste time on any level would never leave me.

As my career progressed, it only became worse. Anyone who has spent more than five minutes in a corporate environment will tell you that time is constantly being measured. What we are doing with our time, how much time we have, and of course my most favorite, how is what we are doing right now, right here, directly related to the bottom line.

It is no wonder we all live obsessed with trying to get a hold on our time. Ben Franklin told us time is money. Like money, none of us thinks we ever have enough of it. Whereas money we can accumulate in the bank to use for a rainy day, time we cannot.

But we need time to make money. We need time to create. We need time to build. We need time to love, play, dream, and plan. So many of us waste our time worrying about not having enough time. We don't know where to start.

When I left the corporate world in 2008 and became an entrepreneur, I found myself challenged. No longer did I have the luxury of someone else's structure to tow the line for me. No one was breathing down my neck, asking me ten times a day how much money we had put on the books in the last hour or whether the new account executive had gotten that appointment with an all-important client. Without someone else cracking the whip, my time was in danger of slipping away without any real productivity.

As a career salesperson, I knew about self-starting within someone else's structure. The challenge would be to keep myself on task within my own.

That's when I remembered the egg timer.

My history with the Egg Timer

The egg timer has been a permanent fixture in my home since I was a kid. My mother had a white plastic Lux egg timer with black numbers she kept on the gas stove in the kitchen. She used it for everything from cooking to keeping track of when it was time for the clothes being washed in the laundry room around the corner to be put into the dryer. Mom even used it for her naps.

We called it an egg timer, but technically there were sixty minutes available on it to parcel out from anything from the three-minute egg to forty minutes for a lemon pound cake.

I learned to like the soft ticking noise at an early age. I never found it a distraction, but rather my own personal sound bite that signaled that a space for something to blossom had been created.

Of course, I was not spiritually evolved enough at that point in my life to understand the concept of creating space, but I felt it intuitively.

The gentle, unobtrusive ticking of an egg timer fell on my ears like the sound of the ocean. Soothing and calming, I grew to understand it as a set amount of time in which something could be created. In the kitchen it was food. On my desk it would be something else.

It started as a way for me to structure my day—a method for me to appropriate out how much time I wanted to work on any given item from writing a blog to networking for new clients. But it became something more. It became a vehicle through which I could design a clean space with which to create whatever it was—my personal oasis in which I might quiet my mind of extraneous interruptions, so I could think and do my best work.

The Greeks have two words for time

In typical Greek fashion, one is never enough, which might have something to do with the fact the ancient Greeks had two words for time: *chronos* and *kairos*. As you might have suspected from the former, *chronos* is sequential time and where we derive the word, chronological. *Kairos*, on the other hand is defined as the right or ideal moment of opportunity.

Chronos is the time our society is obsessed with—the quantity of time, what is happening next, how soon, and how we control it. *Kairos*, on the other hand, is defined as the right moment and is indicative of the quality of that time.

The egg timer, as a time management tool, is designed to get you in that opportune moment, so you can maximize your temporal time.

Sounds silly

I thought so, too. This is why I kept it to myself for a long while. Then came one of those days I didn't know what to blog about, and I decided I would write about my little discovery. The response to that blog was a bit overwhelming, enough so for me not to think this was so silly anymore. People wanted to know where they could buy an egg timer. Then BlogHer picked it up for syndication on their website. My retro tool sparked this light in everyone who heard about it.

Still, every time I suggest it to anyone, I preface that it is going to sound silly, because it does. The idea that a simple timer in the shape of a bright red apple or a yellow billed duck sitting on my desk could possibly be an agent for better time management does sound silly. But I like silly. Silly is often exactly what we need to balance out the seriousness our culture floods us with when it comes to work. Silly makes me smile and often laugh. And laughter is so underrated when it comes to business. Besides, in this case, silly works.

The Basic Principle

The egg timer works on a basic principle. In order to create anything in your life, whether it is writing a book or winning new clients for your business, you need to create a container for that. This requires time and a space within which you want to take the steps to effect your change.

The job of the egg timer is to create that space, uninterrupted and without distractions. You decide what you want to accomplish and how much time you want to spend on it. You set the timer and you don't get up from that desk chair until it goes off.

Not for entrepreneurs only

This concept and this book are not for entrepreneurs only. And by entrepreneur I mean any self-employed individual, business owner, consultant, or writer. It is for anyone who wants to create the openings for more time in their day and to maximize how they are using that.

As a former career salesperson, I know how difficult it is for people locked in a corporate structure to actually carve out the time to do what they love best. Ask any salesperson how much time they are actually selling and they will be lucky if it is as much as 20 percent. It's the same for anyone in management. In today's environment, most are bombarded with paperwork and meetings that get in the way of the real work. This book can help them, too.

Still, I suspect that entrepreneurs are the ones who will most likely pony up a few dollars for a copy for one simple reason. Entrepreneurs tend to think more out of the box and be more open to trying new things. I know this because I have been both a corporate executive and an entrepreneur. Most people I know who live inside the corporate world today will tell you they just don't have the time to be reading about how to manage their time. They are too involved managing their managers or their people or the politics in between. And don't get them started on their personal and family lives. They are likely to think an egg timer sitting on their desk is a sillier idea than I did, one that they will have to explain to their boss who most likely has no time for laughter or whimsical-looking chickens that tick when set to time. But maybe they'll prove me wrong. I'm hoping so.

Whoever you are, if you are reading this, I applaud you for taking a step toward creating the time in which you might have a more enriching life. Not only will this help to open up time in your work day, but subsequently in your personal life.

This is an experiment

Remember this is an experiment, a test drive if you will, to see if it works for you. It's also an invitation to recognize just how much time you really do have and how much more you can create.

If you find yourself already squirming in your seat resisting that possibility, humor me. Take a moment. Set your timer. You have already bought a timer, haven't you? Give me another twenty minutes of your reading time today and see what happens.

Can't I use the timer in my phone?

The timer in your phone is a handy tool for all sorts of things. I use mine in lieu of an alarm clock to wake me up in the morning. However, for these purposes, it will serve as a distraction. Part of what we are trying to do is to eliminate the myriad of diversions we are bombarded with daily, so you can actually accomplish something.

This is what happens when I have tried this with the timer in my iPhone. I start to get a little antsy, especially if I am not yet into the workflow. I want to know how many more minutes I have left before I can get up and go waste some time on Facebook and avoid the work at hand. I pick up that phone to check. For me this requires unlocking the pass code. The next thing I know, I'll notice the text messages I got that I haven't answered. I'll be lured to take a quick peek at my email just to make sure I am not missing anything of real urgency. I'll notice the three phone calls that dropped into voice mail. And before you know it, I am off task. I am thinking about everything else I have to do and manage in the day, but what I set out to accomplish, which at this moment is writing this book.

The purpose here is to dedicate and allot time to a task and to use the timer as our own personal constraint.

Unless you are curing cancer, whatever email or voice messages are accumulating can wait to be answered within a respectable window of time.

What's a respectable amount of time?

My rule of thumb is close of the business day. There will be exceptions if there is a project on the radar that requires a hard and fast deadline, but that is what I adhere to. And because I do, the people who know me personally and professionally do not angst over when I will get back to them, nor do I worry they will. They don't expect in the moment immediacy, but they also know they will not have to wait days for a reply. My reliability allows them not to waste time worrying.

The state of scattered

Most of us today live in a state of scattered thinking. We are pulled in every direction, 24/7, for a share of our time, whether it is the broadcast and cable television networks with their diluted message of "breaking news" or the constant information flowing in our direction via the Internet, social networks, and our smartphones. It is no longer possible to live in an isolated bubble nor would I suggest you do that.

But we cannot let this media-induced fear that we are going to miss something, anything that might make a difference, rule our direction. That fear is exactly what will take us out of the present and off our path. We let those interruptions gain precedence over what we want to and are supposed to be doing, distorting our hierarchy of importance, instead of monitoring our intake on our own timetables.

> **Learning to manage our time to our advantage all comes down to a sense of self-worth and responsibility, to the world and ourselves. It is about knowing and setting our boundaries as to what is best for us.**

Our self-important obsessions

Technology's intent was to simplify our lives. And if used properly, it can maximize our time. I'm a big fan of technology. But one of its big downsides is how it can create the illusion that we are so much more important than we really are.

We go nowhere without our cell phones. In fact, I can break out in a cold sweat if I lose my precious iPhone for one minute in the bottom of my purse. We are connected 24/7, and we interpret that to mean we need to be engaged with it 24/7. If we are not careful, the mobile phone becomes the most important item in our life, instead of the people and work we want to engage with. We get consumed with the busyness it creates and not in creation. Worse, it produces those knots of anxiety in our belly, among the biggest time wasters of them all.

Don't get me wrong. I believe each and every one of us to be important beings on this planet. But our interconnected world that has shown us its benefits in so many ways, also distorts that importance to mean being on call 24/7 to everything and everyone. This is where we can lose sight of what we need to be most engaged with—ourselves, our work, and the people in our lives who are important to us, not our smartphone or our computer.

For the egg timer to work, you will need to shut off the other electronic intrusions that get in the way of the work at hand. If you set the timer for twenty minutes as I do in the morning to catch up on email, you are obviously not going to shut the email off. But you might consider not answering the phone. If your intention is to write your business plan for the next six months, constantly checking your email pings is not going to further the project.

"It's not enough to be busy, so are the ants. The question is, what are we busy about?"

—Henry David Thoreau

I'm really too busy for all this

Another part of this self-important obsession is this idea of "busy." At the moment, it is my number one pet peeve. Ask someone, anyone, right now, how they are and the first thing liable to come out of their mouth is, "I'm so busy." Ask them what they are so busy with and all they can offer is a furrowed brow and one of those exhausted breaths that seems to have been added on for dramatic effect.

By definition, "busy" can be a verb or an adjective. It can be synonymous with occupied, involved, engaged, and concerned.

But it can also denote preoccupied, distracted, diverted, overblown, overwrought, overdone, and fussy.

Most of us when we say we are busy are saying that, because we live in a place that is hectic and cluttered. If our busyness were more positive—being involved and engaged—our response would be specific about the great stuff we are absorbed in. But it's not, because we are too busy to even get that specific.

> **The point of using an egg timer is to busy ourselves with what engages us, not what distracts us from our purpose and our path.**

Take a moment. Write down specifically what kept you "busy" today. Then determine which definition of "busy" it falls under.

I'll have the time to do that when I retire

The first time I heard someone say that was when I was twenty-two years old and a newly minted schoolteacher. The words were uttered by an older colleague in the crowded and smoke-filled teachers' lounge over a tuna fish sandwich. I remember feeling sick to my stomach.

What I heard was that you didn't get to do what you wanted to until you had put in thirty years in the school system. The ready to take on the world young woman I was promised herself then and there that was not how she would live her life. The older and wiser woman has learned that to do that would take focus and discipline.

Discipline

People tell me I am disciplined. It's true. I am. And you are, too, probably more than you think.

Do you take a vitamin every day without fail? Go to the gym three times a week? Never miss an appointment to have your hair colored? Or that Saturday morning tee time at the golf course?

We never look at that as being disciplined, but it is. For some unexplainable reason, when it comes to work, discipline takes on another color palette.

For a long time, I thought being disciplined to be a bad thing. I thought it was very left-brain driven, implying rigidity and lack of ease. Discipline happens when you do something wrong. It's the price you pay for not following the rules.

But I have learned that discipline has a greater meaning. Discipline is at the core of every spiritual practice. Meditation and yoga require discipline to gain any benefit. Championship athletes are winners because of their adherence to their training regimens. Great artists are revered because of their devotion and discipline to their craft. If you want to lose weight, but do not discipline your eating and exercising habits, your weight will remain unchanged. Regena Thomashauer, founder of the School of Womanly Arts, will tell you that even a life of pleasure requires discipline. If you want to write a book, but are not disciplined enough to write even one page a day, the book will never emerge.

Feminine energy embodies the magic of creation. Masculine energy is the discipline exerted to bring it to manifestation. For anything to change, discipline to the craft or work at hand is necessary.

🕐 **The egg timer is a simple tool to bring that discipline in your life.**

Something to "ship"

Seth Godin is one of the marketing gurus that I follow on a daily basis. Seth has written many brilliant books on marketing and the changes in today's work culture, including *Linchpin*.

There are two terms that Seth talks about that are important to mention here. The idea of work as "art" and the idea of having product to "ship."

Seth stretches the concept of "art" beyond the traditional interpretation to whatever your "work" is. "Ship" does not necessarily refer to a product that is going to sit on a truck on the Interstate until it finds a store shelf to call home. "Ship" can mean a blogger sharing an idea by hitting the publish button.

Those are not conventional definitions as this is not a conventional book on creating and managing time. It is a book about unearthing and creating more time in your day to create whatever your "art" is, so you have something to "ship" to your customers. In other words, it's about creating the time for your life.

"How did it get so late so soon? It's night before it's afternoon. December is here before it's June. My goodness how the time has flewn. How did it get so late so soon?"

—Dr. Seuss

Tracking time

I had enough credits to graduate high school early. So that January, instead of going straight to college, I decided to wait until September and took a job as a file clerk at what was then called Bank Americard.

The job amounted to not much more than filing credit card applications. This was back in the day when people used pens and paper and companies kept records in manila folders and not on an imaginary cloud in the sky.

The company wanted to make sure they were getting their money's worth from me, so I had to record everything I did by half hour, right down to how many applications I filed away on a shelf. I was given a 6x8 card on which I recorded the numbers. Before I left the office each day, I was required to turn them in to my supervisor. I learned a lot in those five months. I had a new understanding of the importance of getting a college education, so I was not relegated to filing paper away for the rest of my life. And I learned the importance of tracking my productivity.

Take a moment. For the next week, track what you are doing, by hour. Carry a small notebook with you or keep an excel sheet on your smartphone if that is your preference. Take notes. Start with when you get up and end with when you go to sleep.

At the end of the week, get out the highlighter and see what you notice. How much of your "busyness" was the good kind—focused and engaged—and how much was distraction from real work? Social networking without purpose? Hours of mindless television? Phone calls to commiserate about how you really don't have any time to track your time?

Be sure to include the weekends in your experiment. Time management is not relegated only to our workdays. In the age we live in, we are overloaded with opportunities to waste time, 24/7. Our free time is as precious as our work time. We want to maximize that as well.

Basic Rules of the Egg Timer

- Turn off your email.
- Do not answer the phone unless you are awaiting a call on the cure for cancer.
- Set the timer.
- Do not get up until it rings.

"There is a time for work, and a time for love. That leaves no other time."

—Coco Chanel

Work-Life Balance

Let's be clear. There is no such thing as work-life balance, so if you think the egg timer is the solution, think again. The idea of work-life balance is that it is a destination we arrive at. I don't believe that. Like life itself or love, it is about the journey. In other words, I think of it more as a seesaw.

There are precious moments when it is level, and you really and truly believe you have a handle on it all. But for the most part, one is always weighing more than the other, depending on the hour of the day or the day of the week or the month in the year. The egg timer can assist you to have control over which parts of your life are requiring more attention at any given moment. But work-life balance? If you continue to see it as a destination, the egg timer will not do much to improve upon it.

Alexisms

Alex Tchassov teaches ballroom dancing in New York City. In the midst of teaching the tango or the waltz, he teaches life lessons.

I was not always the easiest student. Drilled into the back of my head was the ballet teacher who told my mother I was "uncoordinated," I would never be a dancer, and my mother was wasting her money and my time paying for lessons. In those days, teachers were not challenged. My mother believed her. Worse, so did I. As a taller than average, skinny young girl, I stretched that untruth to mean I was gawky and clumsy and without a shred of elegance. That idea haunted me into adulthood.

Alex's challenge was to teach me how to dance with this message imprinted in my psyche.

I have a list I kept of what I call Alexism's—moments when he would try to illustrate what he wanted me to do through words.

If you have ever danced, you know that ballroom dancing is about one person leading and the other following and creating the right space between the partners for that to happen with ease and grace.

One of my favorites happened on a day I was challenging his teaching skills. I was in a rush. What else was new? But Alex does not believe in rushing, especially when dancing. He stopped in the middle of the dance floor, pushed his glasses up the bridge of his nose, and spoke in his Russian accent.

"Joanne, you are walking through the door and I have not opened it yet."

His words washed over me in that aha kind of way. My obsession with not wanting to waste a precious moment of our sixty-minute session and to prove that the ballet teacher of my youth might just be wrong had me more focused on pushing than being. All I had to do was pause for a moment and trust. I would have been making more progress than I was by rushing.

We get so caught up in not wanting to waste time, thinking we have to push so hard against the door to get it to open, that too often we get nowhere, both on the dance floor and off.

"We say we waste time, but that is impossible. We waste ourselves."

—Alice Bloch

Creating Time vs. Wasting Time

What if we experiment with a mind shift? Instead of worrying so much about wasting time, what if we focused instead on how to create more time.

WHAT, you ask, am I talking about? Time is finite. We don't get to buy an extra loaf at the store just in case we run out. There are sixty seconds in a minute and sixty minutes in an hour. No more. Of course there are twenty-four hours in a day that multiplies out to 1,440 minutes in a day or 10,080 in a week. This is now starting to sound like an awful lot of time.

Maybe, just maybe, there is enough time within which to do everything we need and want to, and maybe even more.

How To Use The Egg Timer

Whether you are an entrepreneur or sitting in an office run by someone else, the recipe for using the egg timer is pretty simple.

1. Follow the basic rules.
2. Each day you identify what you need to do by making a list.
3. Employ triage to determine what needs to be accomplished first.
4. Decide what needs the twenty-minute rule and what needs a sixty-minute window.
5. Set the timer.

Every day will be different. That is true whether like me, you wear multiple hats of writing, coaching, and speaking or whether you are accountable to a person sitting a few doors away from you. Meetings scheduled by you or someone else are easy to parcel out of your day. But the work that furthers whatever your "art" is—a business, a book, or a new sales prospect—is the stuff that must make it to the top of your daily list or all you will have is a dream and a vision with no movement.

The Sixty-Minute Window

Sixty-minute windows are for the real work. It's a long enough period of time to get into a groove, to create even one really great new paragraph or make at least one good new contact. But it is not so long as to make a person antsy, or after a certain age, a bit stiff from sitting. It is a reasonable amount of time in which to get something accomplished and to feel accomplished. It avoids burnout.

I've always known this intuitively, but apparently for those who need it, there is research to back this up.

Paul Hammerness, one of the co-authors of *Organize Your Mind, Organize Your Life: Train Your Brain to Get More Done in Less Time* says, "Despite all the brain's impressive hardware, there is a limit to what it can deal with." He says most adults can focus on one task for only about sixty minutes. He suggests stopping hourly and walking around, giving your brain time to "reset." I suggest using the egg timer as your reminder and perhaps incorporating in a dance break.

Twenty-Minute Rules

Twenty-minute rules are designed for those things that you need to attend to, but if not careful, will suck you in and take you away from the really important stuff.

For instance, social media. Social media is not the really important stuff. I do believe in it. I see its value, if used with purpose. But on those days when you would really rather not call the ten new prospects on your list, or write the next chapter in your soon-to-be fabulous novel, without a time check, you could while away hours, looking for the boy who sat next to you in the first grade who wrote you a love note and then moved away, never to be heard from again.

Social media is an example of a twenty-minute rule.

Movement

If you think maximizing your time and being diligent about your creation is all about sitting still with a grim look on your face, you are wrong. Make time to move.

When I still lived in my corporate office, I did not have the kind of job that forced me to sit at my desk all day. And even when it did, when I was in a series of meetings or working on a presentation, I instinctively knew those moments when, if I did not stand up and get out of there, I would go out of my mind.

Hourly wage employees are guaranteed a break outside for lunch by law. The self-employed and the salaried are not. They have to create their own laws.

Of course, when we are left to our own limits, we do not trust ourselves. We worry that the fifteen-minute break will turn into thirty, then sixty, perhaps never returning to the project at hand. So it's better not to give ourselves a break at all. Live true to our American puritanical work ethic and toil. Forget time to laugh.

Wrong. If you think you are that unreliable, use the egg timer to time your breaks, too. If it's a really busy day, keep the break time short. Just remember to move.

Rochelle Schieck is the founder of EmbodyQoya, a unique movement designed specifically for women that combines yoga, dance, and sensual movement. In Rochelle's words, "Qoya is based on the idea that through movement we remember." We gain clarity. We get unstuck.

Movement aides in the manifestation of whatever it is we want to create. If we can't feel it, we can talk about it all day long and busy ourselves with tasks that take us off course. The result is we get nowhere.

A walk in the park can help us discover the missing piece of the puzzle in our project or uncover the next line in our marketing brochure. The combination of fresh air and my body moving is often how I get my best ideas. I welcome the technology that allows me to use Voice Memo in my iPhone and record that idea before it slips out of my mind.

Maybe your movement is best served by hitting a bucket of balls at the driving range or an escape to the gym to lift weights. It's whatever works best for you, as long as you move.

A simple ten-minute dance break can yield benefits without straying too far from your desk. It not only gets the blood flowing, it shifts your energy, lifts your mood, and gets you in a better place to meet your deadlines.

I keep a playlist in my iTunes that holds my favorite dance music of the moment. Or I watch one of Rochelle's great ten-minute videos. It's your choice.

Remember you are here to discover what works best for you. I only ask that you take a moment and experiment.

―――――――――――――――

"You will never 'find' time for anything. If you want time, you must make it."

—Charles Bruxton

―――――――――――――――

There really is enough time

We are conditioned to live in a state of scarcity and fear that we are running out of things, of resources, and of time.

I am of the thinking that we have enough time to do whatever it is we want to do. And that we are given by whomever we believe our higher power is, exactly the amount of time on this earth required to do that. But we have to allow for it.

Ever notice what happens when you've had a crush? The adrenaline and hormones are racing so fast that you can't wait to be with that person. Somehow, no matter how "busy" and jammed your schedule was before, you find the time to be with him or her. Instead of dreaming of a hot bath and falling asleep by ten after a long, stressful day, you miraculously find the energy to rendezvous for a late drink.

We make time for what we want to. The thing is we don't always want to. Maybe you don't really want to make time to start that business, or look for a new job, or write that book, or take that pilates class even though you keep saying you do. Or maybe it is just your resistance to change.

"Time is a created thing. To say 'I don't have time,' is like saying, 'I don't want to.'"

—Lao

What are you going to make time for?

Why are you reading this book anyway? Is it just to uncover some new ideas on how to wrap your hands around your time? Are you an entrepreneur fearful about unmanaged time and hungry for a boss of sorts who will tell you how to organize your day? Are you living in a cubicle or a partitioned office dreaming about doing something else, but cannot imagine where you will find the time to do that? Are you a working mom looking to spend more quality time at the end of the day with your daughter? Are you a salesperson trying to find time amidst all the corporate paperwork to do what you love best, selling?

If you could, as Jim Croce suggested in his song, save time in a bottle, what's the first thing you would want to do with your newfound treasure?

The Egg Timer alone is not your answer, but it sure helps

Sitting at your desk one morning and deciding you are going to turn the egg timer on, give yourself a sixty-minute window, and start writing that business plan does not mean you will start your business. It just means you've taken a step. You still have to monitor the outside distractions.

Email

Email is a necessary evil. Whether it is business or pleasure, email is today's preferred method of communication. But what is important to get out of our heads is this idea we have to sit attached to it like a lifeline, not to mention answer each and every one within five minutes of it ending up in our inbox.

When I am really busy and working on a project that involves my undivided attention, like this book, I shut the program down. I check in three times a day—breakfast, lunch, and dinner. I employ the twenty-minute rule. I alert the really important people in my life that if they need me, they better call or text and use a number that identifies them or I will not answer.

This may sound stringent to you. After all, we've developed new forms of addiction to these technologies. And yes, when trying to establish a new set of boundaries, it may bring on the detox shakes. But it's necessary.

🕐 When working on the important stuff, shut down the email program.

Controlling the Inbox

I get a lot of email. Some of it is important. Some is not so. I use a nifty tool called Rules to control where that mail is going. It can be found in your preference folder in iMail if you are an Apple person. Microsoft Office has an option as well.

Here is one way to use this tool. I create folders for my newsletters and label them by subject. For example, business newsletters go to the Business folder, writing to the Writing folder, and shopping to the Shopping folder. I even have one labeled Inspiration for all those inspirational emails I like to subscribe to. I create a Rule that anytime that newsletter is sent to me, it goes directly to the appropriate box.

What happens is these non-critical items bypass my inbox and keep it clean and uncluttered for the stuff that really matters—like when that new client I have been trying to set a meeting with responds, or Oprah sending me a note telling me she's picked my novel for her next Book Club list.

Here technology is not an intrusion, but an asset. It's a feature of your mail program that sorts mail ahead of time. Now when you are ready to catch up on your business news, you open the folder, employ the twenty-minute rule and get to it.

> 🕐 **Manage your inbox, so it does not manage you.**

The Tech Detox Diet

Nutritionists and yogis everywhere advocate periodic detox cleanses. The intention is to eliminate our bodies of the toxins that build up, clogging our intestines and impairing the clarity of our thinking due to bad food choices. We need to do this periodically with technology.

Every now and then, I find myself appalled at our inability to walk without a cell phone attached to our wrist. It usually happens when I am forced to listen to the details of someone's sordid breakup on what would otherwise be a quiet ride across town on the bus. Or the woman in front of me at Trader Joe's the other day, pushing her cart with her child in it, blocking three other customers from the dairy section, because she was too preoccupied with the phone conversation she was having, to notice. Or not being able to cross the sidewalk because the person in front of me is walking while texting, which I personally think is as dangerous as driving while texting.

The scariest part of this is when I recognize myself in the picture. I wonder what happened to just walking without distraction and noticing that the leaves were starting to bud, not to mention the cute guy standing next to me, or that the person waving frantically from across the street is my mother.

That is when I know it is time to go on a tech diet.

The first time I tried this was a couple of years ago. I did it for a week. I set my own set of rules. I resigned myself to only get my news via the actual hard copy of the paper. I limited email to four times a day— morning, noon, end of workday, and before bedtime. I kept myself off social networks except to tweet the blogs I was writing to record my observations.

What I noticed the most was how much more time I had available, and how much freer my mind was to actually think, be creative, and work on what I wanted to work on. The time was there all along. I just hadn't been using it properly. I had allowed the distractions of our society to get in my way.

At the end of the diet, much to my surprise, the world had gone on without me attached to its every movement through Twitter and CNN. So try it. I dare you.

⏱ Take a moment: Create your own version of a tech detox diet and see what happens. Like food choices, we all have those that we are more sensitive to and interfere with our well-being more than others. Let me know how much time you free up.

(The details of my original tech detox diet can be found on ForbesWoman.com)

The Egg Timer as a symbol

The egg timer is more than a time management tool. It is a whimsical item that will make you smile and send out a big signal to you and the universe that you are ready to get to the business at hand. Setting the egg timer right now for another twenty minutes to read the next chapter is making a statement that you are ready to take back the controls of your time and subsequently of your life.

The Yin and the Yang of the Egg Timer

For the world to work properly, we need the Yin and the Yang, that balance of masculine and feminine energies. We all have both within us whether our gender has been labeled as female or male. Feminine energy embodies the nurturing and creative energies that allow something to grow. The masculine energy is what we draw on when we need a structure that establishes boundaries.

I like to think of the egg timer as a symbol of the blend between both. Setting the timer is the masculine mind. The space formed is the feminine in action, designing a container and temperature in which the work will be created.

I'm Not Getting Anything Done!!!

I notice this now and I noticed it when I was still in a corporate office. There are those days when you walk around in circles. There is so much to do, so much information coming in that you just don't know where to start. The more concentric patterns you wear in the carpet, the more frustrated and anxious you get about all you are not getting done.

Take a moment: Turn on the timer. Set it for twenty-minutes. Pick a task, something not too taxing—maybe your expense report. Sit at your desk. Ignore the incoming calls. Turn off email. Do this just until the timer goes off.

The miraculous thing is, even if the report is not finished, you are bound to make progress toward its completion. Acknowledge yourself for having done something and notice how those tensions that had been contributing to the circles ease. The added benefit is that this will fuel you to set the timer for another twenty and then another until you find your groove again. This time it won't be in the carpet.

Forgetting to Acknowledge Ourselves

Another big time grabber is our inability to praise ourselves for the work we have accomplished. Praising is not something we give of easily in our culture, to others or to ourselves. We are much more likely to look for what is not there, than what is. Women have a bigger problem with this than men.

I can still hear my mother's voice stopping herself from complimenting me too much for fear I would "get a big head." I never got a big head. But I do forget, on a daily basis to recognize myself for what I have accomplished.

     ⏱   **The egg timer reminds us it's time to praise.**

I might set the egg timer to write this book for one hour today. In that hour, I might write one thousand words. The next day in that same hour, I might be lucky if I find one hundred more. Both instances deserve my self-praise. In both cases, I sat down, uninterrupted for sixty full minutes to work on my project and made progress toward its completion.

Incorporate the egg timer into an entire day as an entrepreneur and you will feel the surge of energy that being productive elicits. The added bonus is that a sense of accomplishment generally infuses us with the energy to do more.

Taking a Time Out

One of the places adults like to trip up is thinking that in order to maximize our time, we are not allowed to stop. Ever. No breaks allowed. All that results in is burnout and disgust with yourself when you realize you have been breaking your back to get somewhere and are still standing still.

We give our kids a time-out. We tell them to go sit and chill for a bit until they come back to their senses. Yet we don't allow that for ourselves.

🕐   **Go take a time out. Now. Just remember to set the timer, so you don't start lollygagging.**

"Time you enjoy wasting, was not wasted."

—John Lennon

Lollygagging

Lollygagging is something really easy to slip into if you work for yourself. It's not so easy when there is someone just a few doors down you are accountable to. It's one of those old words, only silly people like me still like to use. It's defined as spending time aimlessly—the kind of activity best suited for a day on the East End of Long Island with the waves of the Atlantic crashing at your feet or wandering Paris on a May afternoon.

It's not what you want to be doing when you are building a business, writing a novel, or preparing for a big presentation to your boss.

I admit it. I like to play as much as I like to work, therefore, I make time to lollygag. I would never tell you not to. But when you are wondering why you have not added ten new words to the article you were supposed to finish last week, check that spreadsheet to see how much time you've been lollygagging.

🕐 Play is important. Schedule it, like exercise.

Letting Go of the Time Wasters

If you've been keeping track of exactly where your days have been going, you've no doubt accumulated your own list of what is stealing your time, so much so, that you are convinced you barely have time to read this book.

Now it is time to analyze what gets to go. And only you can determine what.

If you noticed an inordinate amount of time spent watching television, some might suggest disconnecting your cable as a great way to free up time that could be better used elsewhere. But if you are in the business of writing scripts, I suggest not. Watching what the TV networks are picking up and knowing your competition is critical to your business.

Devices such as a DVR come in handy here. I rarely watch live television. An hour's worth of television includes twenty minutes of commercial time. Fast forward those commercials and you have saved yourself a nice chunk of time. Plus, you can watch at your leisure and not when someone else dictates. This gives you better control of your schedule. I know my former colleagues in advertising sales are cringing at this suggestion, but it is a wonderful timesaving trick—unless you are them. For those folks, staying on top of their game requires watching the commercials to see whose spending money in the market. See what I mean about this being an individual food plan?

Social networks are among the biggest new time-wasting culprits out there. They can suck you in and if you have not set your timer, you could while away hours that leave you left with nothing more than a sick feeling as to how all these people you are supposedly "friends" with are creating such fabulous lives and not even one prospect has returned your call all day.

But if you are an entrepreneur with an Internet-based business, you need to be utilizing these networks. They are a vehicle for free advertising and marketing. The trick will be to determine how much time you are going to give to them and to spend it with purpose.

The key with knowing what to let go of and what to better monitor is an individual decision based on your circumstances. There are no hard and fast rules. You know now what your daily overdoses are. You get to write your new prescription.

Multi-tasking is not a badge of honor

I am not sure who decided it was so cool to multi-task. I watched a father the other morning, stopped at a traffic light, texting while pushing his child in a stroller. I saw nothing smart or savvy about that. In fact, I felt rather sorry for his child, that some other person's text was more important to his father than him.

Yes, there are times when you can simultaneously answer emails and talk on the phone. But it is those moments when something is about to go awry. The wrong message gets input. You're too busy typing to hear what the person on the phone was saying and thus unable to make a sound decision.

Multi-tasking is great in the kitchen when you are trying to time the chicken to be ready at the same time as the potatoes. But do not assume it is a great way to manage a workday.

> **Do one thing at a time, give it your undivided focus, and do it right. Ultimately, you've saved time.**

The Timer relaxes

This is another of these moments in this manifesto when you say, "Whaaaaaaa?" Yes, another beauty of the egg timer philosophy is that it relaxes you.

You've set it for sixty-minutes, our optimal amount of time in which to stay engaged and get something done. You've shut everything else off. No interruptions. Now you can relax and not worry about anything else except the work at hand until that buzz jolts you out of your reverie.

About that buzzer

It's not very sexy, or is it very soothing. While I do like the soft ticking sound as each moment arrives, that buzzer can give me a shock, especially when I have fallen into "The Zone" and am creating, creating, creating.

I haven't found an egg timer with a pleasant ring. But I'm working on it. If this book sells well, I may go into the egg timer business and design my own.

Discipline, discipline, discipline

There's that word again—the one we are so ingrained to think of as something bad, something that happens when we have done a wrong.

It doesn't have to be. It can't be if you really want to create anything. Reframe the word. Let it come from a place of valuing yourself enough to find the time to do, not just what you need to do, but what you desire to. Let discipline be a statement of your dedication to you, your art, your family, and your love.

Singers and musicians understand the meaning of discipline, for without practice they would never reach the high notes. But when I say discipline, I know some of you start twitching, hoping for an easier way out.

The truth is discipline can be easy once you've experienced its benefits. When the egg timer and I are one, I feel very accomplished. I did what I said I was going to do. I did not spend my day bantering about the phone calls I needed to make or the pages I needed to write. I made the calls and wrote the words. I took steps. I disciplined myself and it felt really good—so good, that it is not at all hard to set the timer again the next day.

"They say I'm old-fashioned and live in the past, but sometimes I think progress progresses too fast!"

—Dr. Seuss

Isn't an egg timer a bit old fashioned?

Yes, it is. There is nothing hip or hot about it. And yes, there are hundreds of new technologies and apps out there designed specifically with time management in mind. Many may indeed help, but just as many will serve as yet another form of distraction. The point of this book is to create less diversion, not more.

Besides, one of the things that I am passionate about in this fast-changing world is that as we throw out the bath water, we remember the baby is still important.

Mixing up new technologies with good old-fashioned humanity and touches of the non-electronic is an excellent way to move things forward.

The Fear Factor

We live in a fear-based society. We fear terrorist attacks, becoming bag people living in a cardboard box by the side of the road, never finding our one true love, growing old, and falling through a subway grate on the sidewalk. We fear failure and we fear success. Many include God on their list of whom to fear. We fear running out of time.

Some fears are founded and others made up in our head by ourselves or the 24/7 media environment clamoring for a share of our time. Fear can stop us or it can propel us forward.

I like to use the egg timer as an opportunity to use fear to move us forward.

Many of us operate better on a little fear. We fear losing our jobs, so we do the work. We fear getting written up for being late, so we show up on time. We fear getting fat, so we eat healthy.

When implementing the egg timer into your workday, the fear is in the timer itself. Once you decide what you are going to work on in your preferred sixty-minute slot, you don't get to get up until the timer goes off. This is another one of those moments when this sounds pretty silly, but if you imagine that the timer is that boss you used to have down the hall, watching your every move, it will work. Trust me.

"Time is a game played beautifully by children."

—Heraclitus

It's okay to have fun

Most traditional approaches to time management are rather boring. The reason is pretty simple. When we think about work in American culture, we barely crack a smile. We get serious. It is ingrained in us that it is not possible to have fun and work at the same time. Eight hours of working at something you don't like is the necessary evil to the evenings and weekends you live for.

I don't believe that. It's okay to laugh, to smile, and to create ways to make it all fun.

Ever try to get a kid to do something they don't want to? They are pretty quick to display their resistance, the same resistance we keep bottled up inside of us. Trying to be stern and strict just does not cut it. But if we approach it by suggesting we make it fun, offer up ways, however clown-like and nonsensical they may be at the moment, suddenly the child, who moments before was sticking out her lower lip and pouting, is on the task at hand.

If you want to create more time for your life, look for ways to make what you need to do more fun.

Until you value yourself, you will not value your time. Until you value your time, you will not do anything with it."

—M. Scott Peck

Resistance

In his book, *Do The Work!*, Steve Pressfield identifies resistance as one of the forces that works against anyone wanting to create. Resistance refers to fear, self-doubt, procrastination, distraction, and perfectionism among others.

Resistance to living the lives we were meant to live is one of the biggest time-wasters out there. It's the unseen "dragon" that rears its ugly head just when we don't want to see it. This is not a book on the causes of our individual resistance. To really delve into that, I suggest reading *Do The Work!*

But know it exists for all of us, sometimes in our perceived laziness and other times in our feelings of not being deserving of getting what we want.

🕐 Steve Pressfield suggests to *Do The Work!* I will add, with an egg timer within reach.

"The secret of getting ahead is getting started. The secret of getting started is breaking your complex, overwhelming tasks into manageable tasks and then starting on the first one."

—Mark Twain

The To-Do List

There are those who believe it is time to get rid of the to-do list. I am not one of them. In fact, I believe if you are not able to write down what it is you want to accomplish, it will be impossible to achieve it. Combine that with the culture of 2012. With so much information coming at us and so much demanding our time, if you are not writing it down, chances are you will never remember it.

Yes, those who think to-do lists are so yesterday might try to convince you that you will remember the really important stuff. Don't believe them. You will forget. Even when you are crystal clear and on your path with the memory of an eighteen-year old, the Resistance we spoke of before will always try to get in the way of you and your egg timer.

> Whatever your intentions, you must take them to task or you are left with nothing to show for yourself.

Triage

By definition, triage is a term that dates back to the early eighteenth century. It was used by the military as a way of assessing the wounded on the battlefield. Those who needed help most urgently were treated first. But also factored in were their chances for survival.

🕐 As applied to the to-do list in business, you need to assess what is on deadline and what has the greatest chance of revenue hitting the bottom line, both long term and short term.

Ask yourself these questions:

How is what I am doing going to make me money?

How is this task helping to manifest my bigger intentions?

Is it worth setting the egg timer for?

Taking intention to task

Before you can write a to-do list for today, you have to look at your big intentions.

Many will tell you to start with a five-year or a three-year plan. I'm not going to. The world in 2012 is changing too fast to be focused that far ahead of the present moment. What I can do now as an entrepreneur from the comfort of my home office was simply not possible five years ago. How could I have planned for that?

That said, if you really want to create change, you do need to be thinking ahead of today. My suggestion is to start with what it is you want to accomplish over the next twelve months. Give yourself a sixty-minute window for this and sit down in a quiet place and write it out. Get as specific or as broad as you like. Your list may be very long or short and succinct. In any case, the next thing to do is to zero in your Three Big Intentions—the items on that list that you deem most important to what you want to manifest.

Keep The Big Three very visible, every day of the year. One, Two, Three. Near your primary workspace. On your refrigerator. Keep them someplace you can't miss them, no matter how preoccupied you get.

It is from here that you do what I call taking intention to task, by asking yourself what steps you need to take today to create the reality you intend for tomorrow.

My favorite example is the intention to write a book, not just because I have done that, but also because it illustrates what I am talking about with such clarity.

If your intention is to write a book you must write pages, every day or nothing will result. The best intentions in the world that you hold in your vision cannot be realized without doing that work.

Always being clear on The Big Three will make it very easy on a daily and weekly basis to stay on task and know what needs to be on a to-do list.

Some of those tasks will be twenty-minute rules, some sixty-minute windows. It's up to you to decide the specifics by employing common sense and triage.

> Ask yourself right now how what you are doing relates back to your Big Three. If you have an answer, directly or indirectly, you are on purpose. If you don't, find another task.

The Egg Timer as a reminder

Even when I am not so smart as to use it, the egg timer always sits on my desk, ready and waiting for me. It's always there reminding me of what I am not doing and of how easy it would be to break through my resistance.

The Tech Time Stealers

They abound and they surround, with their claws reaching out to distract us for just one instant, so they can lure us in. They are at one moment our friend, allowing us to talk to anyone, anytime from anywhere in the world, and the next our enemy, getting us off task.

They live in cell phones, smart phones, iPads, and computers. They text, email, instant message, and occasionally do something old fashioned like make a phone call and expect us to actually talk. They create whole networks, deemed "social" in which we can, if left to our own devices, waste away hours becoming voyeurs of other people's lives. They are the ugly green-eyed monsters of our own resistance. They are our worry and our fear. They are 24/7 broadcast and cable networks determined to swoop us up into ratings-made fear. They are curve balls that throw our whole day off. They are other people who drain instead of support our visions. They make us stop and wait.

They can control or be controlled. It's your choice.

The Social Media Swamp

The social media swamp can suck you in and swallow you up like the Loch Ness Monster if you let it. Facebook, Twitter, Flickr, Tumblr, Statigram, Instagram, Pinterest, LinkedIn, You Tube, Vimeo, Goodreads, and Shelfari. The list keeps growing. I am a fan of many and see where their usefulness can come into play. As an entrepreneur, you should be using Twitter and Facebook as ways to spread your message. LinkedIn is probably the most useful for connecting to a business prospect or your next job in an organization.

But you have to put boundaries around these or you can find hours disappear as you search to find long-lost relatives.

Social media never gets a sixty-minute window. NEVER. Twenty-minute rules apply here. There's no wiggle room. These are new addictions like those to alcohol, drugs, food, and sex and left unchecked will send you to rehab.

Many solopreneurs see these sites as virtual water coolers. As a businessperson, you need to utilize them with purpose. What are your reasons for being there? To make a new business connection? Promote your blog or your product? Catch up on news?

🕐 My rule is to get on these sites no more
than twenty minutes at a time, no more
than four times a day.

I like to use the old radio daypart theory, which was
that different people listen at different times of the
day, so you should employ equal parts of what they
call "dayparts": Morning Drive being between the
hours of 5:00 a.m. to 10:00 a.m., Daytime 10:00 a.m.
to 5:00 p.m., Evening Drive 5:00 p.m. to 8:00 p.m.,
and Nights 8:00 p.m. to 12:00 midnight into your
advertising campaigns.

This works for social networks as well. Different people
are utilizing them at different times of the day. This
approach is especially helpful if you are using them to
reach your potential customers.

Waiting

Waiting is a time stealer—waiting for something big
to happen instead of continuing to take your steps.

In selling, there is no waiting. A good salesperson
learns early on not to wait for anything, but instead
to keep moving, looking for new prospects to keep
the sales funnel full. But even the best salesperson will
wait for that one big order to close, or the contract

on that book, or the studio to pick up the options on the script, or the money to come through from the investors you pitched last week.

We all catch ourselves getting so attached to the outcome that we waste time, as we wait patiently with our hands folded for its arrival.

🕐 **Don't wait for the call. Let it go. Pick something else to work on, and there is always something else, that circles back to your Big Three. Set the timer. Don't get up until it rings.**

"The bad news is time flies. The good news is that you're the pilot."

—Michael Altshuler

Worry

Worry can grab a hold of your time in the most unproductive way possible. It changes nothing. It infiltrates your energy field. It feels horrible. It makes us anxious. It squanders time with nothing left to show for it except more worry.

We are fed a lot to worry about in the course of a day. We worry about money, about the economy, about health care costs, and terrorist attacks. We worry we've gotten too old to change anything much less try something new. The media offers up promotional teasers all day long that work on our worry genes just so we will tune-in to their news clip. Too often we are fed new versions of the truth, just to make us worry that we are all going mad.

Right now I'm worried I'll never get this done on time, and I'm the one who set the deadline!

> The best solution for worry is to remember that you can do something, no matter how small, that will make a difference.

Pick something from your to-do list—something on the relatively easy side that doesn't need your brain's full attention until you've warmed it up. Then reach, and this will be hard, but reach over to your egg timer and see if you can remember how to set it. All that worrying may have you forgetting how.

Be gentle. Maybe this isn't time for the sixty-minute window. Give it twenty and see if you can start to refocus that worry energy to actually doing something that makes a difference in your little section of the world.

"The only reason for time is so that everything doesn't happen at once."

—Albert Einstein

The Curve Ball

You know these. The day is looking great. You are moving along at a good clip, getting everything done you intended to. And then it comes—the curve ball. It's a phone call, an email, or a letter. It's something you didn't expect that takes you off plan. Maybe, it even disappoints you. And now you are frozen in your tracks.

While writing this book, I had a curve ball. I got the first pages of the critique back for my next novel. The bottom line? It needs a lot more work than I had bargained for. In fact, the wording was something that would have sent me immediately to a bottle of vodka when I was still trying to figure out if I was indeed a writer. It threw me off course. It wasn't what I wanted or expected, so I lost a few hours. Okay, maybe a whole day. It's going to happen. It will always happen. Time will get wasted, often when you least expect it or want it to. The key to managing those moments is to be aware and recognize that you might need to call a time out.

Always keep that egg timer in plain sight, so you know the easiest route to getting back on track.

The Energy Vampires

You know who they are—those people who not only interrupt your day, but also sap your energy. Some take it for their own. Others just rest theirs on yours like a thick cloud of smoke that makes it hard to breathe. If they're really good at what they do, they are capable of leaving you physically unable to move.

These are the people who will tell you all the reasons something won't work or something is wrong, without offering a viable solution. They see everything as impossible. Their conversation and banter block you from the task at hand. They are the people who sit in the jobs they hate and are convinced the world will end yesterday. Their energy can be toxic. It will throw you off track if you let it.

Removing energy vampires from your life is not always easy. Often they are family members whom you cannot simply shut out of your life. But there is one thing you can do.

> Set the timer when the energy vampires appear. Give them twenty minutes. No more. And then send them on their way. Maybe even give them this book.

Don't answer the phone

When I was a kid, no one ever thought not to answer the phone. If it was ringing, it was assumed it was something important. We had only one phone in our house that sat on the wall in the kitchen. There was no call waiting. If you called someone who was already talking to someone else, you got a busy signal. Today that is something that only occurs if you dial the home of someone over the age of eighty.

Caller ID did not exist, nor did voice mail. So, it made sense if the phone rang to answer it. You were encouraged to keep phone calls short, so as not to "tie up" the line. No wonder it seemed as if we had more "time" then. We did. We had less intrusions and diversions.

Technology has changed all that.

> **The phone is no longer a novelty, which means you don't have to answer it all the time. It's not always important, especially when you've set your timer and are trying to get something done.**

Yes, if you are a neurosurgeon on call, answer the phone, no matter what. But if you are a business person having a meeting with one of your people, answering every call that comes in only serves to waste time for both of you.

The Periodic De-Clutter

One of the things that grabs our time is what I like to call the pile-up. When the clutter around you starts to overwhelm you and suffocates. Sometimes that translates into all those "chores," the simple tasks you let slide by, while you were focused on the important stuff. Sometimes, it is actual paper—you know, those things that get stuffed into a folder, so you can look at them later or shoved into a closet, so you don't see them and can pretend they do not exist.

> Scheduling a periodic de-clutter affords you another opportunity to open up time and space in your life.

Of course, most of us put off the "spring cleaning" of our closets, because we don't have the time, see it as not important, or we are too fearful that once into it, nothing else will get done.

But if you schedule in periodic de-clutters, an hour or two a week, in which you hit one closet at a time, even just the sock drawer, you will be keeping that energetic space around you free from unnecessary clutter that might just be what's getting in the way of your creativity and productivity.

As always, set the timer. These are never longer than a sixty-minute window.

Meetings

No matter if you work for yourself or for someone else, meetings are inevitable. If we are not careful, they become time wasters, instead of sources of productivity and leave us with little to show for ourselves that we can actually "ship" somewhere.

Always set a beginning and an end time for meetings and let whoever is participating know what they are. My rule of thumb for groups is a sixty-minute window and for individuals a twenty-minute window. If a group meeting warrants more than an hour, give a break after each sixty-minute window or you will lose the engagement of who is there, consequently wasting everyone's time.

Setting meeting boundaries is also helpful for those people who want our time, need our time, deserve our time, but if we are not careful, will take all of our time.

Set the timer at the beginning of a meeting with one of your team. Let them know in advance the amount of time they have and no more. Give them your undivided attention, and then send them on their way.

"It is the time you have wasted for your rose that makes your rose so important."

—Antoine de Saint-Exupery, *The Little Prince*

Go wander

Wait. Didn't I say before not to lollygag? Isn't that what wandering is? Not exactly. Lollygaging is aimless. Wandering is with purpose, sort of. And if incorporated into your day properly, it can create magic.

Some days I get stuck. Who doesn't? The patriarchal viewpoint is to tough it out. My viewpoint is that sometimes you can't. Sometimes you have to get up, leave the office, and go wander—with purpose.

I know. I've confused you. Say you are working on your new website. You like it, but something is not right with the visual and you just can't pinpoint it. You like the verbiage, but it is just not making you sing. You set the timer. You stared at it for an hour and you got nowhere.

This is when wandering can come in handy. Leave the office with that visual in your mind and let it percolate. Some of my very best ideas have come forth when I am smack in the middle of Central Park, wandering. Note here never to leave the technology at home, because this is where it comes in ever so handy. You can record your brilliance right into Voice Memo, so it is not lost forever into the ether. You can snap a picture of what you saw that set off that creative spark. You can even use a handy little App called TurboScan that lets you snap a picture of a wordy document you find in your travels and email it to yourself as a PDF.

🕐 **There is alchemy in wandering. Go create some magic.**

Napping

Yes, it's true. Naps are good for you. Naps make you more productive. The idea of plodding along when you are suffering exhaustion, just because you have to, so you can brag later how hard you worked is another of those patriarchal culture misnomers. It's easy to nap if you work from home. It's not so easy in an office unless you work for a forward-thinking organization like *The Huffington Post*, which has nap rooms for its employees.

Sleep is important. When you are exhausted and you can't string more than three words into a coherent order, you know it is time.

Go take a nap. Just remember to set the timer. Twenty minutes is the optimum amount of time to nap and leave you refreshed. More will defeat the purpose.

"Now is the moment that never ends."

—Deepak Chopra

Meditation and Ritual

If anyone had ever told me that meditation might open up more time in my day when I was deep in the throes of my corporate life, I would have laughed out loud. But it does. As few as fifteen minutes of quiet time each day to focus on your breath and gather your energy from the myriad of places it escapes to creates oceans of time later in the day.

You design your ritual, however it feels best—a bit of the day, just for you, to be quiet and gather your energies. Moments generated to just *be*. I have always found mornings best, before the rest of the world wakes up. But you might find a mid-afternoon break better—or if you really have a handle on your time, both.

Light a candle. Stretch on a yoga mat. Do whatever feels most comfortable to you, as long as you sit and focus on your breath and emptying your mind, instead of filling it with the to-do list. You'll get to the to-do list later.

In this land of unfocused and scattered energies we live in, a daily ritual that includes meditation is the only hope we have to hold our own. You can even set the timer—five minutes at a time until you work your way up. Or find a guided meditation that works for you, like the one Agapi Stassinopoulos, author of *A Dose of Greek Wisdom*, makes available on her website.

> Take a moment. Now. Sit, close your eyes, and focus on nothing but the fact that you are breathing.

Setting Deadlines

I wrote my first novel while I still held a demanding corporate job. When people ask me how I did that, I do stop and wonder myself. The truth is when I started writing it, I didn't even know it would be a novel. I only knew that writing made me feel whole and made the nine to five part of my life easier. I had to write in order to breathe. So, I found a way to carve out just enough time each week. I hadn't yet employed the egg timer, but I did use another trick.

I joined a writer's group that met every second Tuesday. Each meeting I was supposed to bring ten new pages to share at the workshop. I've always been a good student and one able to make deadlines, self-imposed or not. So, I played on what I knew about myself and each Tuesday we met, I had ten new pages. Or else.

My "or else" meant I couldn't go to the workshop, which at that point in my corporate career was like taking away my life preserver.

Some weeks, my pages were great and some not so great. But what is true in writing is true in so many creative efforts and by creative I include business here. Often the road to a great finished product is not about how good each step along the way is, but that you are taking them and they are moving you forward.

> ⏱ **Even if you break them, setting deadlines will get you where you want to go.**

Getting up early

I started getting up early when I lived in Washington, DC. It was at one of those more stressful times in my career when I was the general sales manager of a CBS-owned radio station that had no ratings, that industry determinate for how much you could charge for a commercial spot. The company had just been purchased by Westinghouse, and a corporate culture struggle for power made for pressure-filled days.

There are two ways to manage that kind of stress. Alcohol and exercise. I chose both. It was pretty easy to fit in the time for alcohol. Exercise was more challenging, given the amount of time one can spend sitting in his or her car when living inside the Beltway. My only option was mornings.

That experience taught me to love getting up early, those moments of solace, as the city is waking up, that allow you time to gain control of your thoughts and your day before they control you. I still get up early, even though my commute is just a walk into my living room.

> (Ⓣ)   Getting up early gives you an edge. Whether it is to exercise, to meditate, or to get a head start on your inbox, you've given yourself a gift.

Exceptions

Good rules are like the blueprint for a house. You can't really build anything without them. But that doesn't mean they can't be tweaked and still work.

In fact, if you get so caught up in adhering to the rules and not in understanding why they were established in the first place, they've defeated the purpose.

The basic rules of the egg timer are to:

- Eliminate distraction
- Set boundaries
- Stick to them
- Pay attention

Beyond that, adjust according to individual preference.

"You've always had the power"

When Glinda, the Good Witch, speaks these words at the end of *The Wizard of Oz* Dorothy asks why she hadn't told her before. Glinda's reply is that she knows she wouldn't have believed her. Dorothy needed to discover that by herself.

My hope is that by this point in the book, I've led you down your own yellow brick path and you've discovered what you already knew. All the time you need to do what you must do and what you want to do is there for the taking. It always has been. You just have to organize for it.

"This time, like all times is a very good one, if we but know what to do with it."

—Ralph Waldo Emerson

What will you do with your time?

You've bought your egg timer. You've made it to the last page, so you are at least slightly convinced it is indeed possible for you to create more time for your life. In fact, you are certain that even if you employ just a few of these ideas, you have unearthed more time than you could have imagined.

So my questions are:

What will you do with that time?

What changes will you make in your life?

What is that one thing you were convinced before you had no time to do, you will now take a step towards?

What is next for you?

I want to know.

Acknowledgments

I might never have taken the time to write this book if not for the encouragement of the posse of friends I am blessed with, who point out to me on a daily basis that I know how to get things done and that others could benefit from learning how I do it.

Nancy Moon, Amy Aho, and Julie Kilbane, your never-ending support and stand for me are what gets me to believe in me. Karen Quinn, your creative genius gave me the title for this book. Laura Wood, there are no words for what I have learned from your teachings. My never-ending thanks and love to you all.

To my mother for showing me the way from the start. And of course, to the egg timer. Who knew I would ever write a book about you?

About the author

Joanne Tombrakos has a genetic predisposition to organization and being a self-starter. This served her well in her professional career, first as a public school teacher and later as an advertising sales executive working for companies that include CBS and Time Warner. In 2008, she left that behind to become an entrepreneur. The new challenges she faced are the genesis of this book.

Today she is a writer, coach, and speaker as well as the author of a novel, *The Secrets They Kept*. She blogs on living and working after corporate America at http://onewomanseye.blogspot.com

She and her egg timer reside in New York City.

For more information or to contact Joanne, please visit www.joannetombrakos.com